I am with you always, even to the end
of the world. Matthew 28:20

ISBN: 979-8-9922853-5-2- Paperback

NBeirene Press

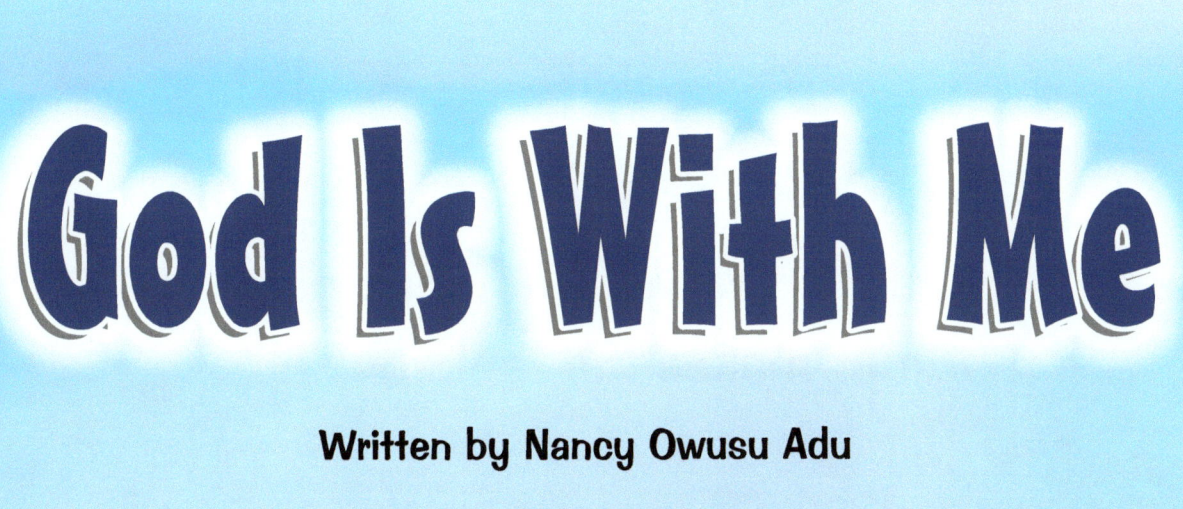

God Is With Me

Written by Nancy Owusu Adu

God sees Me

I can't hide! He will always find me.
Even in a crowd, God sees me and
that makes me feel special!

From Heaven God looks and sees everyone. Psalm 33:13

God hears Me

No matter the noise, God still
hears when I talk to Him.

Every wish, every whisper
reaches His ears.

The Lord hears us when we call on Him. Psalm 34:17

God thinks of Me

**God's thoughts of me are precious
and dear.**

**His thoughts about me are far
better than anything I can imagine!**

*I know the thoughts I think towards you; thoughts of peace
not of evil, to give you a hope and a future. Jeremiah 29:11*

God teaches Me

When I don't know what to do, He shows me how.

Even when I want to do things my way, He teaches me a better way- His way.

I will teach you the way to go; I will advise you as I keep my eye on you. Psalm 32:8

God blesses Me

God's blessings can't be measured in a cup! Like rain,

He pours His blessings on me everyday!

God is able to bless you with more than you need so that you can help others. 2 Corinthians 9:8

God cares about Me

He cares when I'm up, He cares
when I'm down.

He cares about how I feel and
what I think!

Cast your cares on Him because He cares.1 Peter 5:7

God loves Me

God loves me like no one can, in ways I can't explain.

Nothing beats God's love. It's a love like no other.

God showed His love for us in this way, even while we were sinners, Christ died for us. Romans 5:8

God speaks to Me

At times He whispers, other times
too He nudges my heart.

If my ears stay open, I will hear
when He speaks!

*When you call on me, I will answer you and show you great
things you don't know. Jeremiah 33:3*

God leads Me

As He leads, I follow.
He only leads me on the
best path for me.

He leads me in the paths of righteousness for
His name's sake. Psalm 23:3

God provides for Me

Even before I ask, God knows exactly what I need and in no time, it shows up!

God will give you everything you need according to His riches in Glory through Christ Jesus. Philippians 4:19

God forgives Me

No matter how big or small the sin,
God always forgives and never
brings it up again.

I forgive your sins and remember them no more.
Isaiah 43:25

God knows Me

God knows me better than anyone.
He knows the good and the bad,
but loves me the same.

You know my sitting down and my rising up.

Psalm 139:2a WEB

About the Author

Nancy Owusu Adu is a Christian writer, a wife and mother of 3. With over 2 decades of experience teaching Sunday school, Nancy is passionate about bringing God's Word to life for both the young and young at heart. Among her published Children's books are titles such as God's Word Is, Jesus Gives Me, Who is Jesus to me, and many more. Outside of writing, Nancy enjoys reading, traveling, and connecting with family and friends.

Follow Nancy to stay connected

Instagram @ nancy.owusuak

Facebook @ Nancy Owusu Adu

www.ingramcontent.com/pod-product-compliance
Lightning Source LLC
Chambersburg PA
CBHW041607120626
46551CB00002B/347